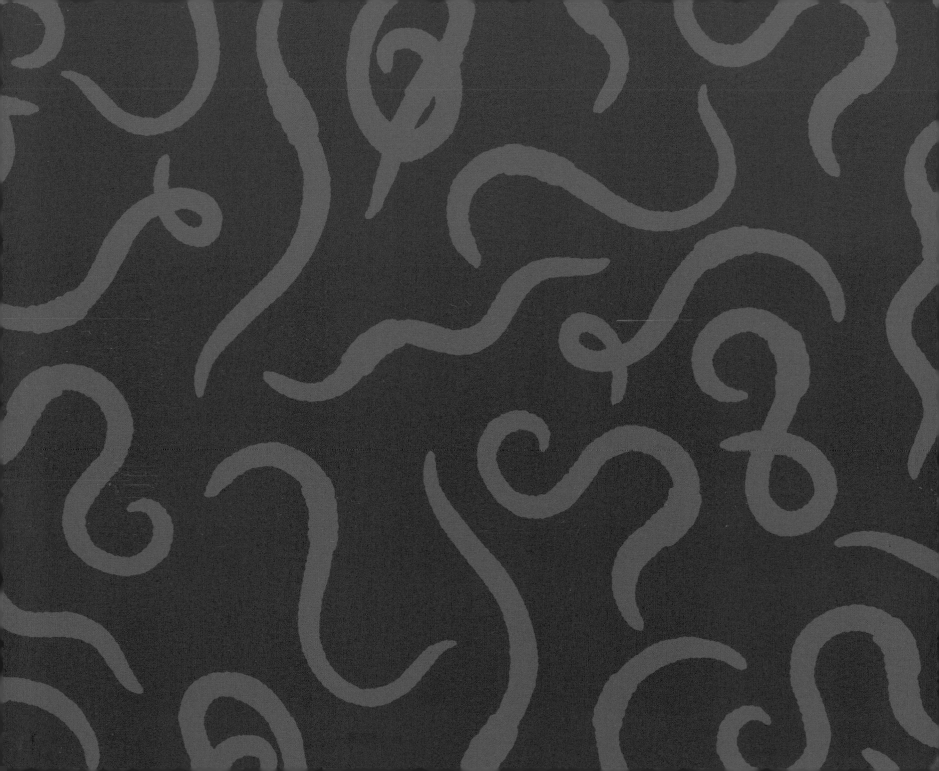

LET'S-READ-AND-FIND-OUT SCIENCE®

STAGE 2

Wiggling Worms at Work

by Wendy Pfeffer • illustrated by Steve Jenkins

HARPERCOLLINSPUBLISHERS

For all children who enjoy wiggling worms
—W.P.

Special thanks to Dr. Stanley Green of
Penn State University for his time and expert review

With thanks to Dr. Edwin Berry from Iowa State University and Barbara
Bromley, Mercer County Horticulturalist, for sharing their knowledge of worms
with me. My sincere thanks to Sarah Thomson for her expert guidance.
—W.P.

The *Let's-Read-and-Find-Out Science* book series was originated by Dr. Franklyn M. Branley, Astronomer Emeritus and former Chairman of the American Museum-Hayden Planetarium, and was formerly co-edited by him and Dr. Roma Gans, Professor Emeritus of Childhood Education, Teachers College, Columbia University. Text and illustrations for each of the books in the series are checked for accuracy by an expert in the relevant field. For more information about Let's-Read-and-Find-Out Science books, write to HarperCollins Children's Books, 195 Broadway, New York, NY 10007, or visit our website at www.letsreadandfindout.com.

Library of Congress Cataloging-in-Publication Data
Pfeffer, Wendy.
Wiggling worms at work / by Wendy Pfeffer ; illustrated by Steve Jenkins.
p.   cm —— (Let's-read-and-find-out science. Stage 2)
Summary: Explains how earthworms eat, move, and reproduce and how they help plants to grow.
ISBN 0-06-028448-X ——ISBN 0-06-445199-2 (pbk.) —— ISBN 0-06-028449-8 (lib. bdg.)
1. Earthworms——Juvenile literature. [1. Earthworms.]   1. Jenkins, Steve, 1952- ill.   II. Title.   III. Series.
QL391.A6 P48   2004   2001039519   592'.64——dc21

Typography by Elynn Cohen   18 SCP 20 19 18 17 16 15 14   ❖   First Edition

Wiggling Worms at Work

Down in the ground, under your feet, thousands of worms wiggle around flower bulbs and tunnel under trees. They twist and turn, eating almost anything in their way. These wiggling worms are at work.

Farmers plow their fields to loosen the soil. Crumbly soil lets the roots of plants spread out and grow. Worms also loosen the soil as they wiggle along. They are called nature's plows.

As worms twist and turn, they push aside loose soil. This creates tunnels. Air flows along these tunnels. Rainwater trickles down. Roots drink it up. Moist ground helps plants grow better.

Worms tunnel in hard-packed soil
by swallowing it. The soil goes in the
worm's mouth, slides into the crop,
then passes down to the gizzard.

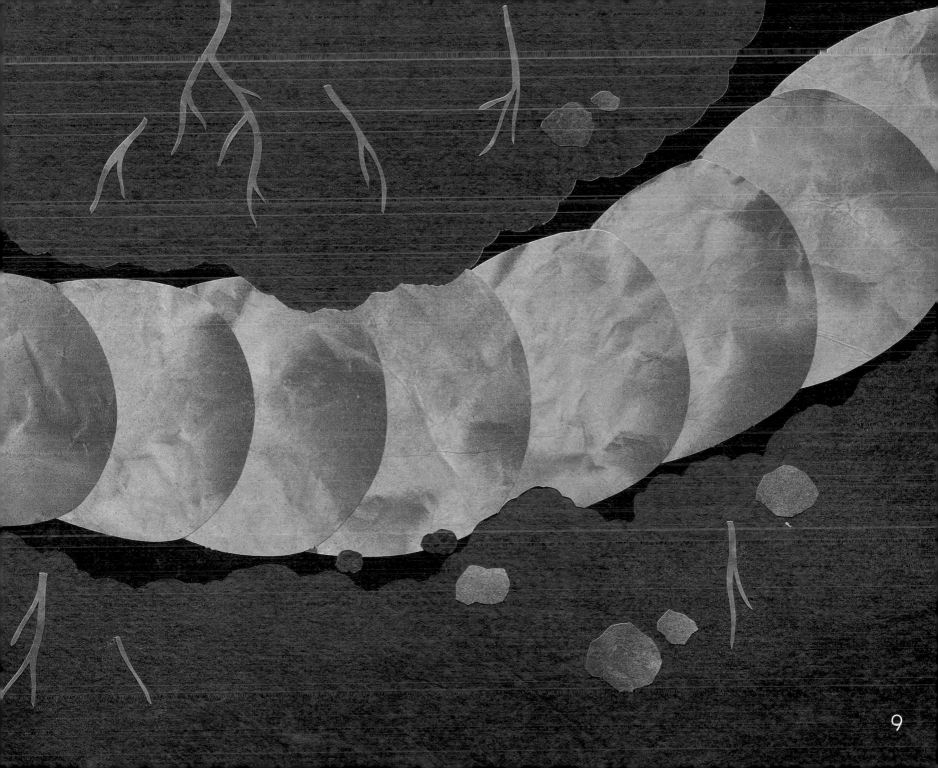

Worms do not have teeth. Muscles, fine grains of sand, and small stones in the gizzard grind the soil. Worms digest leaf and plant bits that are found in soil, just as you digest a salad.

What's left passes through a worm's body and comes out its tail end in the form of pellets, called worm castings. These castings make good plant food. They help fruits and vegetables grow bigger and better.

Sometimes worms crawl above ground.
When they tunnel back down into the
ground, they pull dead leaves and plants
down with them.

These plants make the soil better as they rot. Seeds come down, too. Some of these seeds send out roots. Seedlings sprout. Worms help new plants begin to grow.

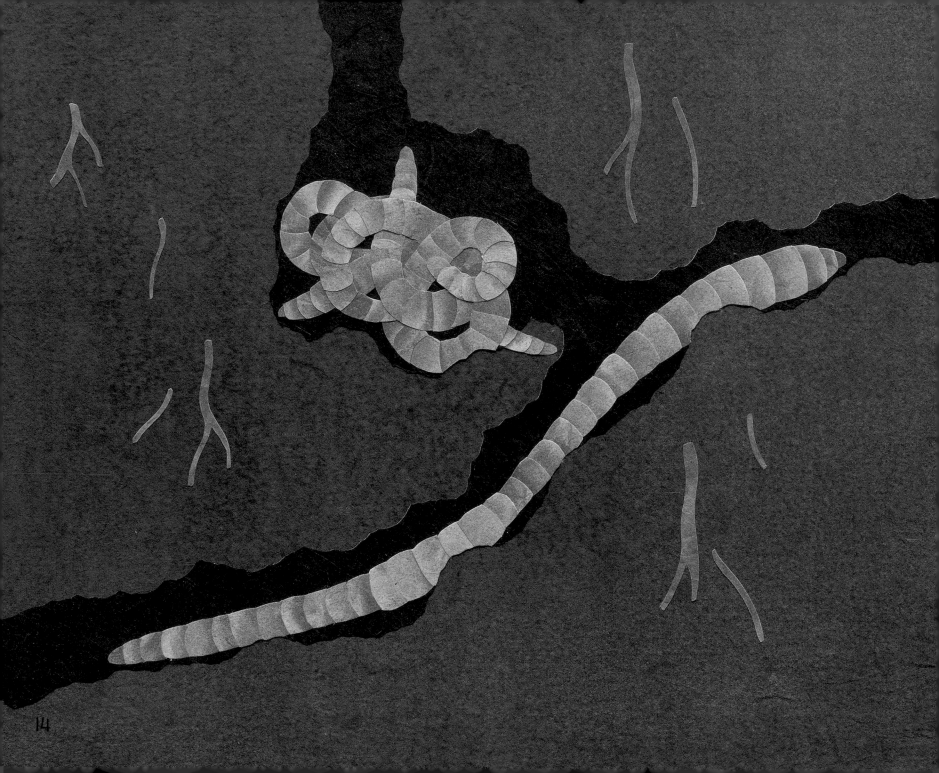

14

Worms can wiggle, twist, turn, and even tie themselves in knots because they have no backbones. Their soft bodies are made up of rings, or segments. These segments act like the coils on a Slinky toy. They let a worm bend.

A worm has no legs, but eight bristles under each segment act a little like legs. They help a worm move. Strong muscles allow the worm to stretch out its front end. It becomes long and thin. Then the worm fastens its front bristles to the soil. The back end slinks up, making the worm short and fat.

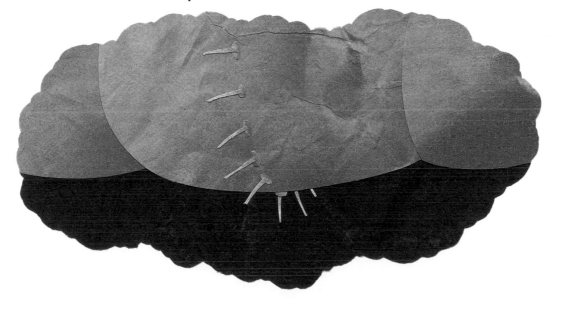

16

The worm wiggles along, stretching and slinking, stretching and slinking. With all its wiggling, twisting, and turning, it's a wonder a worm knows where it's headed. It has no eyes, no nose, no ears, and hardly any brain at all.

But a worm knows what's happening nearby. It feels vibrations on the ground and senses a hungry robin. Quickly the worm slips back into its burrow. Hiding is the only way it can protect itself from enemies.

Worms also hide from the sun. They must live in damp soil since they breathe air through their moist skin. In the hot sun their skins dry up and they can't breathe.

Sometimes worms crawl to the surface to find food. They select dead and decaying plants to drag back to their burrows. These plants contain bacteria that worms eat. Healthy plants do not. Worms pick leaves with pointed ends rather than round ones. No one knows why.

Worms also eat fungi and mold. They slurp the hairlike strands of mold the same way you might slurp strands of spaghetti.

Worms eat at the entrance of their burrows. Then each worm covers any leftover plants with its castings. This pile of worm castings is called a midden. It hides the top of the worm's burrow and acts like a door to keep out bad weather and rain.

In spring, before the weather warms, worms wiggle to the surface to mate. Worms are different from most other animals. Each worm is both male and female. But each one still needs a mate. After mating, each worm crawls back into its burrow.

When the weather cools, a ringlike cocoon forms near the head of each worm that has mated. Slowly, the worm begins to move backward. The cocoon inches forward on the worm's body just as a ring on your finger would move.

The cocoon passes over openings in the worm's body. Up to thirty eggs slip out of the openings and into the cocoon.

In a few minutes the cocoon slips off the worm's head, just as the ring would slip off your finger. The ends of the cocoon close. Inside the cocoon the eggs are fertilized.

In about three weeks the eggs hatch. Out of about thirty eggs, only three or four wormlets emerge from each cocoon. They look like tiny pieces of cotton thread, less than an inch long. But they are fully developed worms and live completely on their own. They do not need their parents' help.

The wormlets inch along, finding bits of dead plants to eat, dragging them to their tunnels, and covering any leftovers with their castings. They wiggle underground, loosening the soil and making tunnels. Even tiny wormlets help the soil.

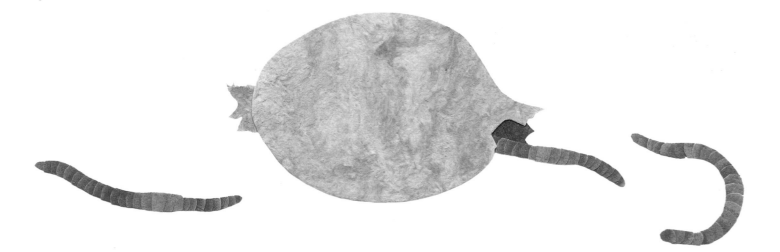

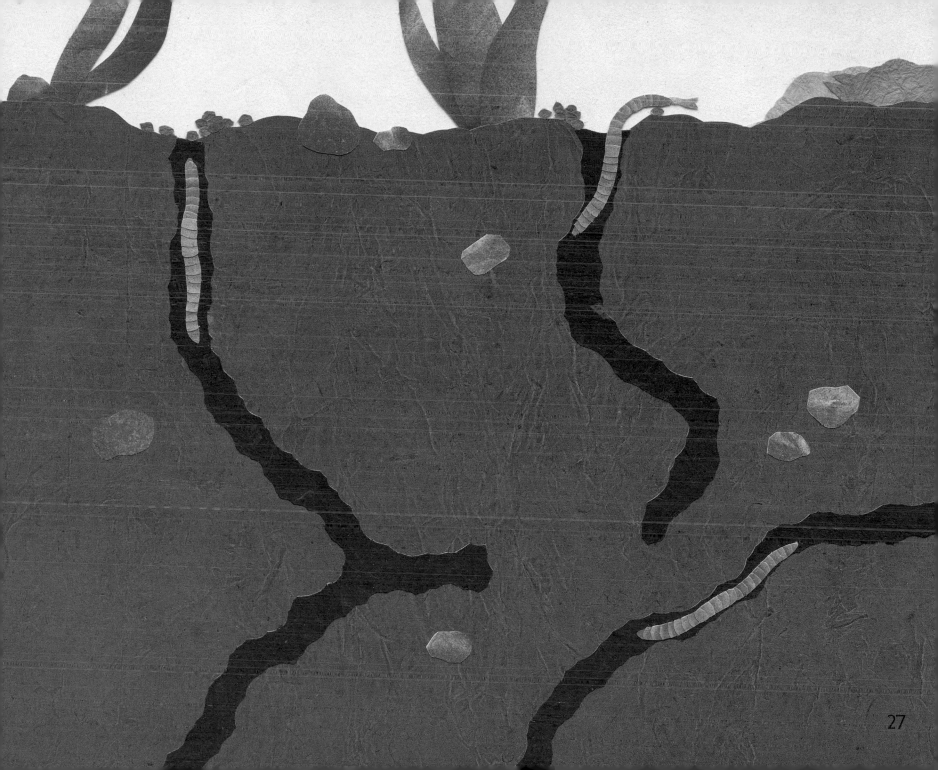

These babies grow fast. In six weeks they are adult worms.

In winter, the soil near the surface freezes. The worms plug up their tunnels and move down to warmer soil. They stay there until spring. Then they wiggle up, tunneling, twisting, and turning, until they're right under your feet again.

Vegetables and flowers grow better. Trees grow bigger. Grass grows greener, because there are thousands of wiggling worms at work.

FIND OUT MORE ABOUT WORMS

- A Worm of Your Own

1. Find an earthworm. The worms you are most likely to find in North America are called night crawlers. Go outside after a rain and look for a night crawler on the ground. Or go out at night with a flashlight to find one. You can also buy night crawlers at a fishing supply store, such as a bait and tackle store, if you can't find them outside.

2. Examine your worm. Feel the rings on its body. See how it bends so it can wiggle, twist, and turn.

3. Carefully pull the worm through your fingers. Does it feel smooth and slippery from head to tail? When you slide your fingers from its tail to its head can you feel the bristles?

4. Watch how your worm uses these bristles to walk. Put the worm on your arm. Feel how it fastens the bristles onto your arm. See it stretch out long and thin to move forward. Then see it pull its back end up. Now your worm is short and fat, but it will be long and thin as it moves forward again.

5. Be sure to let your worm go. Place it in a moist spot.

6. Draw pictures of how your worm walked. Then draw pictures of different ways that other animals move (by swimming, flying, hopping, etc.).

• A Worm's Home

Find the entrance to a worm's tunnel by looking for its castings. Place some dead plants nearby. Cover the area with a box. Peek each day. Watch a pile of castings form strange shapes.

• Do Earthworms Really Help the Soil?

Try the following experiment to see whether earthworms really make soil rich. You will need:

2 flowerpots	seeds (Any kind will do. Pumpkin seeds,
soil from your yard	watermelon seeds, grass seeds, or
castings from outside a worm's tunnel	lima beans will all grow fairly easily.)

1. Fill one flowerpot with soil.
2. Fill the other with soil and add the castings.
3. Plant seeds in each pot.
4. Put both flowerpots in the sun.
5. Water the plants equally.
6. Take notes each day on how the plants grow. Which plant grew bigger and better?

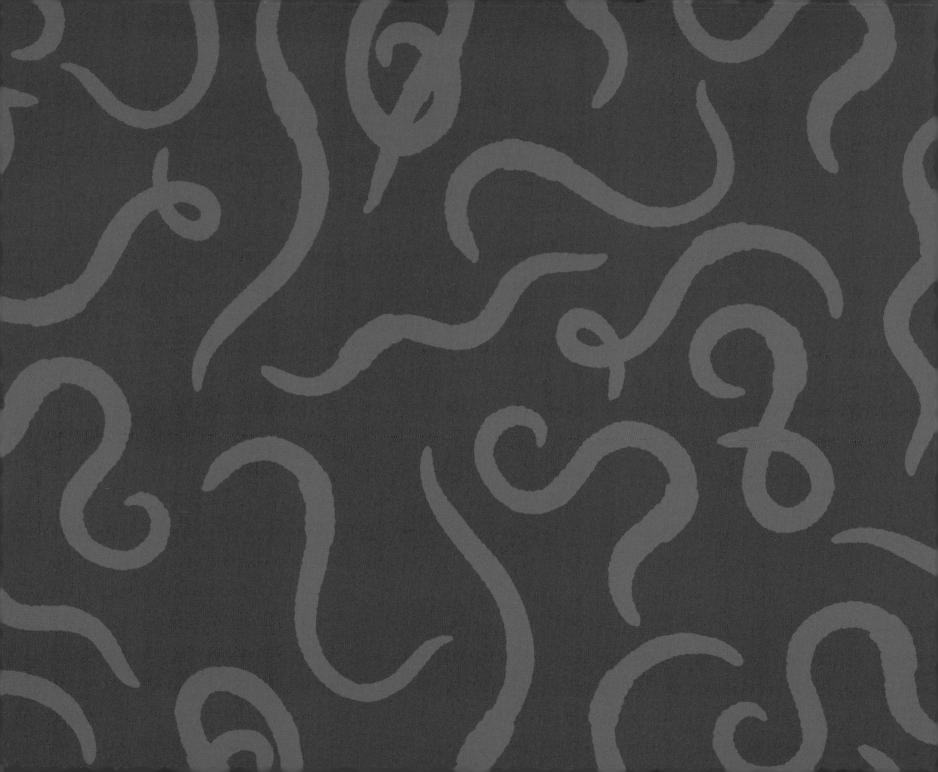